CW00505619

Original Title: Twilight Musings

Editors: Theodor Taimla
Autor: Karoliina Kadakas
ISBN 978-9916-748-82-4

Twilight Musings

Karoliina Kadakas

Celestial Chimes

Upon the night, the heavens ring
With melodies the stars do sing
The moonlight's dance on silken streams
A symphony of ancient dreams

Through twilight's veil, the echoes drift
A cosmic tune, a timeless gift
Each note a whisper from afar
Guided by a distant star

The planets hum in soft accord
A harmony we can afford
To lose ourselves within the night
And chase the sound of pure delight

Veil of Stars

Beneath the veil of starry night
A tapestry of silver light
The cosmos paints a vast expanse
With glittering threads, they weave and dance

Galaxies like whispered tales
Of timeless lore, of cosmic sails
Sailing through the endless sea
Of twinkling lights and mystery

In every corner of the sky
A glimpse of wonder, clear and nigh
The veil of stars, a sight to see
A boundless realm of fantasy

Gathering Shadows

As twilight fades, the shadows grow
A gathering of night's soft glow
They whisper secrets, dark and deep
And in their cloak, the world does sleep

The moon arises, pale and bright
Amidst the gathering of night
Its silver beams, a gentle guide
Through the darkness far and wide

In shadowed corners, dreams take flight
Born from the quiet of the night
The gathering shadows hold the key
To realms of endless fantasy

Night's Embrace

In night's embrace, we find our rest
With stars above, we're truly blessed
The gentle whisper of the breeze
Carries the songs of ancient seas

The moon's soft glow, a beacon true
Illuminates the midnight hue
It casts its spell on earth below
In night's embrace, we come to know

A world of dreams, a silent space
In night's embrace, a warm and safe place
To close our eyes and voyage far
Guided by each shining star

Candles in the Dark

Flickering flames in shadows deep
Softly dance where silence weeps
Light waltzes on a solemn breeze
Bringing warmth with gentle ease

In the night, their glow persists
A beacon through the mists
Hope's tender glow does mark
These small candles in the dark

By their light, we find our way
Through the darkest parts of day
Ever burning, ever bright
Their steadfast flame our guiding light

Whispered Eves

Soft whispers of the twilight near
As the day whispers farewell dear
The breeze carries tales untold
Of dreams and nights of old

Stars emerge, their secrets share
With the moon in silent prayer
Each glow a story left behind
In the stillness of our mind

Night wraps the earth in tender care
Whispered eves, beyond compare
Hushed and gentle, soft they weave
The magic of these whispered eves

Glimmering Twilight

As twilight falls, the glimmer starts
A dance of light that warms our hearts
Colors blend in a soft embrace
Painting skies with tender grace

The horizon blushes, night descends
Daylight's song its weary end
In the balance of dusk's soft glow
A peace that only twilight knows

Stars awaken, blink in cheer
Glimmering light both far and near
In this tranquil, gentle rite
The world basks in twilight's light

Quiet Crescendo

In the hush of evening's breath
Quiet solstice steals our breath
Nature hums a gentle tune
Beneath the rising silver moon

Soft sounds grow, a symphony
Of night's calm serenity
The world turns in sweet suspend
As day and night begin to blend

What was still now gently sings
Carried on soft, whispering wings
This is life's unfolding show
The beauty of the quiet crescendo

Whispers of the Night

In the hush of restive shadows
Softly curls the evening breeze
Murmurs secrets, ancient echoes
Through the boughs of silent trees

Stars like lanterns in the distance
Glimmer, whisper glowing tales
Moonlight drapes a silver instance
On lanes and river trails

Crickets sing in murmured chorus
Owls glide on silent wings
Night unveils its hidden forests
Where the quiet twilight clings

Sunset Soliloquy

Embers glow on western sea-line
Heaven's palette bursts to flame
Clouds in gilded hues entwine
As the day and dusk proclaim

Skies of amber, gold, and crimson
Cotton candy colors bloom
Whispers fade, the light grows dimmer
Yielding to the night's dark plume

Softly fades the sun's last shimmer
Stars emerge in twilight's sweep
As the world in blush grows dimmer
Nighttime's lullaby we keep

Cloak of Evening

Cloak of evening softly falling
Drapes the earth in twilight's sheen
Veils of shadows start their calling
Whispers calm where light has been

Lost within the dusk's embrace
Moon and stars in dance align
Mystic hues of violet grace
Every corner, every line

Silent night attends her calling
Curtains drawn with darkened thread
In her arms we keep on falling
'Til the dawn calls out ahead

Starlit Contemplations

Beneath a dome of starry glimmers
Thoughts alight and spirits soar
Infinite, their distant shimmers
Echoes of what came before

Boundless skies invite reflection
Mysteries without a sound
Every star a pure connection
Threads of light that all surround

Night reveals such contemplations
Underneath this vast expanse
Stars engage with our sensations
In their patterned, gleaming dance

Transient Glow

Morning dew on petals bright,
Whispers of the fading night.
Sunrise paints the sky aglow,
Transient moments swiftly flow.

Winds that carry stories old,
Secrets in the dawn unfold.
Fleeting light of early morn,
In its wake, new hopes are born.

Echoes of the twilight gleam,
Vanishing like a lucid dream.
Colors merge, then softly fade,
In the transient glow displayed.

Nocturnal Thoughts

Stars above in silent gaze,
Guide the mind through shadowed maze.
Whispers of the darkened hour,
Moments hold a special power.

In the quiet, thoughts take flight,
Wandering through realms of night.
Moonlight casts its silver thread,
Knitting dreams as we lie in bed.

Night's embrace, a velvet shroud,
Covering the world's loud crowd.
Thoughts like fireflies in the dark,
Glowing with a hidden spark.

Afterglow Visions

Sunset hues in skies unwind,
Leavings of the day behind.
Shadows stretch and softly blend,
Colors in the night descend.

Golden rays of dusky light,
Greet the coming of the night.
Mirrored in the evening's bay,
Afterglows of passing day.

Phantom dreams on twilight's breath,
Whisper softly, facing death.
Visions hold, then slowly part,
Lingering within the heart.

Deepening Shadows

Twilight's veil begins to fall,
Casting shadows on the wall.
Dusky whispers fill the air,
Shadows deepen, everywhere.

In the dimming, secrets hide,
Lost within the eventide.
Light retracts its golden beams,
Melting into midnight dreams.

Softly fades the sun's last spark,
Welcoming the coming dark.
In the depths, the silence grows,
With the deepening of shadows.

Gloaming Whispers

The sun dips low, the sky ablaze,
A canvas painted with twilight's brush.
Whispers of night begin their praise,
In stillness, hush by hush.

The trees sway gently with the breeze,
Leaves murmur secrets, tales untold.
Nature's symphony, moments seize,
In twilight's grip, the world unfolds.

Shadows lengthen, day recedes,
Soft whispers gather in the air.
Gloaming whispers, silent creeds,
Wrap the earth with tender care.

Evening Reverie

Golden hues and amber light,
Dance upon the evening's grace.
Stars prepare for their quiet flight,
As day yields to night's embrace.

Crickets sing their timeless song,
Echoes through the cooling air.
Moments linger, pure and strong,
In twilight's tender, gentle glare.

Memories drift like autumn leaves,
Caught within the evening's fold.
Reverie in the dusk, one believes,
In stories, whispered yet untold.

Fading Sunlight

As the sun descends, a fiery ball,
Splendor spreads across the sky.
Fading sunlight casts its thrall,
Bids the world a soft goodbye.

Rippling waters catch the glow,
Mirrors to the day's retreat.
In fading light, the stories flow,
Moments precious and bittersweet.

Nighttime's promise in the air,
A gentle call to dreams anew.
With fading sunlight, none compare,
To the magic twilight drew.

Veil of Night

The veil of night begins to fall,
Stars embroider the evening's cloak.
Mysteries whisper, shadows call,
In the stillness, dreams evoke.

Moonlight silvers every leaf,
Casting spells upon the land.
In the night, one finds relief,
Guided by the moon's soft hand.

Veil of night, a sacred shroud,
Wraps the world in deep repose.
In its embrace, dreams speak loud,
While the night serenely grows.

Glimmers at Dusk

Golden hues paint the sky's whispering light,
As day softly surrenders to the night.
Shadows lengthen, dreams begin to weave,
In twilight's embrace, heart must believe.

Stars awaken, casting silent, twinkling spells,
While secrets the dusky air gently compels.
Hope rides the winds of the cooling breeze,
Whisperings of dusk put the soul at ease.

Luna's Symphony

Underneath the silver beams, softly they lay,
Moonlight dances on the gentle bay.
Whispers of the night, a lullaby serene,
Nature sings her song, in a world between.

Crickets chirp, the nocturnal choir begins,
Each note harmonious, brings peace to skins.
In Luna's gaze, the world finds its song,
A brief moment where we all belong.

Crimson Horizon

Fiery strokes paint the horizon's edge,
A burning blaze where day meets pledge.
Birds whisper farewells under crimson skies,
As the sun takes its leave, the day stifles sighs.

Mountains shadowed in an amber glow,
Reflection of the world, with secrets to bestow.
Dreams are sparked in the evening's light,
Reddens the sky, a mesmerizing sight.

Nightfall Narratives

Stories whisper through the night so calm,
In moon's embrace, a soothing balm.
Mysteries unravel under starry shrouds,
As night tells tales, enchanting the crowd.

Silent paths under nocturnal skies,
Twinkling lights with a thousand eyes.
In each breath, the night weaves lore,
Endless narratives forevermore.

Shades of Dusk

Evening stretches, paints the sky,
Whispers secrets, winds draw nigh.
Birds to nests, their songs subdued,
Twilight's peace, in colors hued.

Shadows lengthen, soft they creep,
Day to night, begins to seep.
Stars emerge, in heavens wide,
Moonlight waltzes, oceans tide.

Crickets sing a gentle tune,
Underneath the watchful moon.
Silence deep, a calming rust,
Nature's breath in shades of dusk.

Dreams at Dusk

As the daylight bids adieu,
Skyline drapes in twilight's hue.
Dreams awake, on horizon's brink,
Stars igniting, night to link.

Wanderers of night's embrace,
Seek their paths in velvet space.
Quiet whispers, hearts unlock,
Guided by the ticking clock.

Mysteries in shadows thrive,
Magic pulses, dreams arrive.
Dusk unveils its secret door,
Begging us to dream once more.

Nocturnal Reflections

Moonlight spills upon the ground,
Silent echoes all around.
Reflections of the day gone by,
Twinkle softly in the sky.

Thoughts of moments, hearts once shared,
In the night, emotions bared.
Darkness cradles tender dreams,
In its depths, the silver gleams.

Stars, like memories aglow,
In the silence, truths bestow.
Night, a canvas vast and deep,
Locks our secrets, safe to keep.

Evening Serenade

Wind caresses, cool and soft,
Whispers sweetly, floating aloft.
Meadow flowers, gently sway,
In the evening's tender play.

Melodies from streams afar,
Blend with twilight's first bright star.
Harmony in night's embrace,
Peaceful tunes in thoughtful grace.

The world, in quiet, sings its song,
Laughter settles, dusk grows long.
Hearts and minds in love pervade,
Underneath the evening shade.

Ephemeral Nightfall

A whisper in the waning light
Waltz of shadows, soft and slight
Moonrise kisses day's farewell
Stars in secret stories tell

Hushed murmurs of the evening breeze
Rustling through the ancient trees
Night's embrace, a fleeting dance
Ephemeral, in haunted trance

Luminous dreams in velvet skies
Ethereal glow in twilight eyes
Time suspends in muted sighs
As nightfall draws its silver ties

Moments blend in darkened hue
Softly fades the evening blue
Peace descends, a gentle call
In the ephemeral nightfall

After Sun Silence

Golden beams retreat in grace
Night descends with tender pace
Whispers hum in silent choir
Daylight wanes, its final fire

Shadows stretch in silken veil
Softly speaks the evening tale
Harmony of dusk and night
In afterglow of fading light

Quietude in every fold
Mystic hues in twilight's hold
Silent stars in silent skies
Gleam above as daylight dies

Crickets sing in tender tone
Echoes of the day now gone
Restful calm in night's expanse
In after sun's serene silence

Halcyon Twilight

Gentle whispers of the dusk
Cloak the world in evening musk
Golden rays in twilight's hue
Bathe the earth in soft adieu

Calm descends on weary land
Peace bestowed by twilight's hand
Day to night, a seamless flight
In the halcyon twilight

Birdsong fades in soft refrain
Crickets sing their evening hymn
Shadows lengthen, softly blend
As the daylight finds its end

Quiet settles, peace prevails
Stars emerge in glittering trails
Harmony in twilight's sight
In the halcyon's embrace of night

Resting Light

Sun bids farewell, whispers low
Twilight's gentle, soothing glow
Fades into the arms of night
Peaceful is the resting light

Shadows dance in silent grace
Moonlight kisses every place
Stars awake in velvet skies
Soft repose in night's disguise

Evening hums a tender tune
Cradled by the silent moon
Tranquil streams in silvered beams
Flow within the night's soft seams

Dreams entwined in restful sleep
Memories in twilight deep
Harmony in evening's sight
In the quiet resting light

Stars' Conversations

In the quiet night, they gleam and sway,
Whispering secrets far away.
Ancient tales, both old and true,
Twinkle softly in the blue.

Guiding travelers through the night,
With their gentle, shimmering light.
Silent promises they keep,
While the world below, in sleep.

Constellations form above,
Telling stories of old love.
Heroes, myths, in cosmic dance,
Captured in their timeless trance.

Each star a voice, clear and bright,
In the tapestry of light.
Conversing through the endless sky,
As the world in darkness lies.

Eve's Silent Serenade

Hush of dusk, the day takes flight,
Soft hues blend with approaching night.
Shadows stretch as light retreats,
Evening's song, so soft and sweet.

Crickets chirp in twilight's grace,
Moonlight paints a silver trace.
Breeze whispers through leaves' array,
Night unfolds in silent sway.

Stars emerge in gentle streams,
Dreams unfold with midnight's gleam.
Night's embrace, a soothing guise,
Underneath the velvet skies.

Whispers of the day's goodbye,
Followed by the night's soft sigh.
Nature sings in muted tones,
Eve's serenade in twilight's home.

Dimming Horizons

Sunset drapes the sky in red,
Day's last light, in silence spread.
Golden hues begin to fade,
Night's soft murmur, now conveyed.

Mountains cast their long, dark shades,
Twilight's glow in fleeting trades.
Horizons blend in twilight's hand,
Ending day with hues so grand.

Birds retreat, their songs now still,
Gentle cooling, evening's chill.
Stars prepare to take their place,
Bringing calm and gentle grace.

Dusk transforms the light to gray,
Nighttime whispers, shadows play.
Horizons dim as night descends,
Day in quiet beauty ends.

Shadowed Reflections

Mirrors hidden in the night,
Cast in moon's reflective light.
Shadows dance on silent walls,
Whispers echo through the halls.

Silent steps in darkened rooms,
Echo soft through twilight's glooms.
Reflections of the past arise,
Caught beneath the starlit skies.

Shades of memories, soft and clear,
Lingering thoughts of yesteryear.
In the night, their forms appear,
Bringing moments, distant, near.

Through the shadows, truths are seen,
In a night's reflective sheen.
Depths of silence, dark and deep,
In the shadows, secrets keep.

Gazing into Dusk

The sky becomes a canvas wide,
Brush strokes of gold, the sun's last pride.
And in this moment, time feels still,
A whispering breath, a gentle chill.

Birds retreat to silent nests,
As moonlight's charm subtly suggests.
Shadows lengthen, soft and deep,
Cradling earth in calming sleep.

Stars awaken one by one,
A prelude to day's end begun.
With watchful eyes we stand and trust,
The secrets whispered into dusk.

Evening's Breath

Beneath the sky, the world unwinds,
In twilight's arms, soft breeze reminds.
The day lets go, an easing sigh,
As evening's breath bids light goodbye.

Candles flicker in windows low,
Soft music in the distance slow.
Each note a gentle, flowing sound,
Embracing all the lives around.

Fireflies dance in whispered flight,
Adding sparkle to the night.
Beneath their glow, the world finds peace,
In evening's breath, all worries cease.

Twilight's Kiss

Upon the edge of night's abyss,
We feel the touch of twilight's kiss.
The warmth of day begins to fade,
As shadows form a soft parade.

Colors blend in hues of grace,
A tender smile on evening's face.
With every touch, the light transformed,
By twilight's kiss the night is warmed.

A gentle calm envelops all,
Around the world a silken shawl.
In this embrace, we find our rest,
Held gently to the twilight's breast.

Silent Hues

The paint of dusk in silent hues,
Draws forth the night on nature's cues.
A tapestry of stars unveiled,
In silent hues, night's tales are trailed.

Mountains rest in shadows dark,
Beneath the sky's celestial arc.
Whispers follow evening's veil,
In silent hues, new dreams set sail.

Rivers mirror dusk's soft light,
As day surrenders into night.
In silent hues, we find our way,
Guided by the twilight's sway.

Dim Light Ruminations

In the hush of evening's breath,
Shadows stretch and softly blend,
Thoughts like whispers tread with stealth,
In the dusk, my mind attends.

Silent specters of the night,
Gently dance in twilight's hold,
Mysteries clothed in gentle light,
Stories of the past unfold.

Candles flicker, shadows play,
Dreams awaken with a sigh,
In this half-light's tender sway,
Time slips gently, drifting by.

Echoes of the sun's retreat,
Paint the sky with hues of grace,
In the fading, bittersweet,
Contours of a long-held place.

Twilight Whisperings

Whispers ripple through the air,
As the day begins to fade,
Softly, whispers everywhere,
Twilight's gentle serenade.

Crickets sing their evening song,
Moonlight dances on the stream,
In the twilight hours long,
Life becomes a waking dream.

Stars ignite the velvet blue,
Night unveils its hidden lore,
With a whisper, dark and true,
Secrets linger, evermore.

Breath of twilight in the trees,
Rustling leaves, a lullaby,
In the quiet, hearts find peace,
'Til the dawn lights up the sky.

Sunset Meditations

Resting sun in crimson robe,
Kisses earth with tender flame,
In its glow, the world enrobe,
Twilight dances, soft and tame.

Golden hues in twilight's art,
Brush the sky with soft embrace,
In this canvas, hearts impart,
Thoughts of love and endless grace.

Shadows wane, the light succumbs,
Whispers weave through evening's prance,
Silent peace, like beating drums,
Guides us in a twilight trance.

As the day bids sweet adieu,
Dreams arise in twilight's glow,
In the calm, reflections true,
Moments tender, ebb and flow.

Day's End Contemplations

Sunset's glow, a fleeting glance,
Paints the sky with fiery hues,
In the twilight's soft expanse,
Moments blend in crimson views.

Breezes whisper through the trees,
Quieting the day's last breath,
In the stillness, thoughts release,
Dreams awaken from their rest.

Silver moon ascends the night,
Stars align in cosmic thrill,
Day's end brings a soft respite,
Hearts find solace, quiet and still.

Memories of day now past,
Gently woven in the dark,
In the night's embrace, they last,
Flickering like a lantern's spark.

Sun's Farewell

The sun dips low, its warmth to end
In twilight hues, the sky it sends
A whisper soft, the night descends
In golden waves, the day suspends

Crimson shades in skies apart
As daylight fades with gentle art
A cloak of stars, the night imparts
In tranquil peace, the heavens start

A final glow, a fleeting gleam
In twilight's hold, like a dream
The world in hues of amber beam
A symphony, the evening theme

The shadows stretch, the light grows thin
As dusk embraces all within
An orchestra of crickets sing
In harmony, the night begins

Sepia Skies

Beneath the sepia sky, we stand
A world transformed, dissolving sand
Time unfolds with gentle hand
In amber tones, the twilight planned

The edges blur, the day transcends
In roseate ways, the light descends
A moment held, where calm extends
In sepia skies, our hearts, it mends

The evening whispers secrets old
In copper tales, the night unfolds
A mystic dance, the stars behold
In twilight's grasp, the world is told

The sepia hues, a curtain drawn
To greet the night, to meet the dawn
In quiet peace, where dreams are spun
Sepia skies, a day well done

Glistening Dusk

In glistening dusk, the day retreats
A silver glow, as time completes
With shadows long, the night it greets
In twilight's bow, the stars it meets

The sky adorned in twilight's hold
With hues of pink and threads of gold
In quiet grace, the world enfolds
A gentle kiss, the night unfolds

The breeze it whispers, soft and light
In dusk's embrace, the first of night
A canopy of dark and bright
In tranquil waves, the end in sight

The moon ascends, a watchful eye
In glistening dusk, the world sighs
A velvet quilt of starlit sky
In twilight's arms, the night arrives

Crescent Contemplations

Beneath the crescent moon we lie
In silver light, the evening sighs
A tapestry of gentle sky
In quiet thought, the night implies

The crescent whispers tales untold
Of ancient dreams and stars of old
In cosmic dance, the night unfolds
A silent story to behold

The stillness speaks in softest tone
In crescent light, we're not alone
A universe in shadows shown
In whispered winds, the night condones

In crescent's gaze, we find our peace
A tranquil space, where thoughts release
Amidst the stars, our souls at ease
In night's embrace, our hearts increase

Veil of Evening

As sun dips below the vast plain,
Colors splay on skies unfurled.
Crimson, gold on twilight's gain,
A veil draws on the waking world.

Whispers float on the evening's breath,
Mysteries in silence yearn.
Stars ignite in the heavens' depth,
Their tales in endless burn.

Shadows stretch in tranquil hue,
The day's embrace now gently ends.
Moonrise casts a silver view,
Night upon the earth descends.

Night Breeze Thoughts

Soft whispers in the cooling air,
Secrets that the darkness tells.
Minds wandering, thoughts they bear,
Caught in night's enchanting spells.

Leaves rustle in the quiet night,
Singing songs of ages past.
Under stars, the mind takes flight,
In the breeze that travels fast.

Dreams are woven in night's loom,
Threads of hope, fear, and wonder.
As the world beneath the moon,
Finds a place to softly ponder.

Afterlight Musings

When the sun has left the sky,
And the colors fade to dreams.
Silence weaves its gentle sigh,
In the moon's reflecting beams.

Thoughts are born in twilight's hush,
Moments lost and futures bright.
In the afterlight's calm rush,
We find wisdom in the night.

Stars align in paths unseen,
Guides through darkness, ever wise.
In the quiet, minds convene,
Sharing secrets of the skies.

Horizon Reveries

On the edge of day and night,
Where dreams and reality blend.
Horizon spreads its gentle light,
A promise at each day's end.

Hopes and fears in layered haze,
Painted lines of golden hue.
In the twilight, minds do gaze,
At horizons far and true.

Every ending brings a start,
In the cycle, life renews.
With the horizon in my heart,
I find paths that I choose.

Ephemeral Twilight

The sun dips low, in twilight's gentle grace,
A fleeting moment caught, time's tender chase,
Shadows elongate, kissing night so sweet,
Day whispers softly, in twilight's retreat.

Colors merge in hues of purple and gold,
Stories of the day, in silence unfold,
Birdsongs fade, in lullabies of night,
Mystic twilight, an ephemeral delight.

The sky, a canvas of dreams never told,
Embracing night, in its navy blue cold,
Stars peek shyly, in the vanishing light,
Ephemeral twilight, bidding day goodnight.

Twilight Whispers

The evening's hush, a symphony so low,
Wind's gentle breath, through leaves begins to blow,
Twilight whispers, secrets of the soon-to-be,
Night's silent call, a whispering decree.

Crickets start their song, a twilight choir,
Echoes of day fade, kindling night's fire,
Soft murmurs to the moon, by shadows cast,
Whispers of twilight, both first and last.

Dim light stretches like fingers through the trees,
Caressing the earth, stirred by gentle breeze,
Moments of dusk hold whispers tight,
Twilight weaves stories, into the night.

Stars and Solitude

Night unfurls, a blanket rich and deep,
Stars awaken from the daylight's sleep,
Solitude whispers in the moon's soft glow,
A realm of peace, where quiet dreams flow.

Each star a guardian of the night's embrace,
In solitude, they line the sky's vast space,
Silent companions to the wandering soul,
Stars and solitude, make the night whole.

The world lies hushed beneath a sapphire dome,
Finding solace in the starry poem,
Midnight confessions in solitude found,
Stars listen gently, to each sacred sound.

Evening Grace

The day winds down in evening's warm embrace,
Shadows dance, leaving day's hurried pace,
Golden light, painting the earth so fair,
Evening grace, whispering a tender prayer.

Birds flying home, tracing lines in the sky,
The world slows down, as night draws nigh,
Whispers of the breeze in a soft, tender sway,
Evening's grace, leading night into day.

The moon ascends with a silvery light,
Stars join hands in the velvet night,
Nature bows in the evening's soft lace,
A tranquil tribute to the evening grace.

Soft Night's Song

Beneath the moon's tender glow
The whispers of stars arise
Silent melodies drift below
In the vast, starlit skies

Soft winds weave dreams unseen
Through the shadows that gently caress
Night blossoms, serene
In its velveteen dress

Crickets hum a sweet refrain
A lullaby in the night's embrace
Echoes in the midnight rain
Gentle as a lover's grace

The world in slumber sighs
Wrapped in twilight's tender shroud
Whispers of the night softly rise
In dreams, where silence is loud

Rest, oh weary heart, do lean
Into the night's soft song
Until dawn's first gleam
In its embrace, where you belong

Dusk's Silent Echo

As the day fades into twilight's hue
Whispers of the evening emerge
Shadows dance to a tune anew
In the horizon's gentle surge

The sun bows in a blaze
To the night's sweet, tender call
Colors in the sky set ablaze
Before the darkness falls

Birds sing the day's final notes
In a chorus gentle, low
As twilight gently floats
In an indigo glow

The stars peek from their haven
In a nightly silent show
An echo of the day's haven
In the night's quiet flow

Dusk speaks in hushed tones
In moments solemn, slow
And in its embrace, we're not alone
As dreams begin to grow

Memories at Sundown

The sun dips low, a crimson fall
Memories wake in the soft, warm glow
Whispers of days we recall
In the fading light, tender and slow

Golden hues kiss the sky
Remnants of laughter, smiles that gleam
In the quiet, our spirits fly
Chasing the twilight's dwindling beam

Shadows stretch, a timeless dance
Stories unfold in the dusky light
In these moments, we find our chance
To relive days as day turns to night

The fragrance of the past, so sweet
In twilight's arms, we find the way
To the echoes of those we meet
In the sunset's gentle array

As night's curtain softly falls
With stars, memories align
In this silence, our heart enthralls
In the twilight, where past and present entwine

Evening's Silent Symphonies

The sun retires, a day's sweet end
And the evening sings its silent song
With twilight, shadows blend
And the night-time hours prolong

Stars emerge in radiant arcs
A symphony of quiet light
Embracing the world's darker parts
In the tranquil hush of night

The breeze whispers secrets old
Through leaves and ancient trees
Stories of dusk softly told
In the cool, evening breeze

Moonlight paints a silver sheen
On the tranquil, quiet scene
In the still, serene routine
Where peace and night convene

In the symphony of the night
Harmony breathes a gentle sigh
Soft notes in the moon's light
In the silent night's lullaby

Midnight Murmurs

In the stillness of the night,
Whispers soft on breeze take flight,
Stars above in silent dance,
Bedtime tales of sweet romance.

Moonlight casts a silver thread,
Dreams and wishes gently spread,
Hushed the world in calm repose,
Secrets only twilight knows.

Cicadas sing their lullaby,
Night unfolds its velvet sky,
In the shadows, whispers play,
Hints of dawn's first light of day.

In the heart of midnight's grace,
Tranquil moments we embrace,
Beneath the canopy of stars,
We find peace, and all that's ours.

Murmurs fade with coming morn,
New day's light, a promise sworn,
Yet within our hearts remain,
Midnight's whisper, soft refrain.

Glimpse of Night

Night's tapestry, dark and deep,
Dreams within its silence sleep,
Stars like lanterns gently beam,
Guiding us through twilight's seam.

Shadows dance in moonlit glow,
Whispering secrets we don't know,
Owl's call through ancient trees,
Carried far on evening's breeze.

Crickets chirp in rhythmic song,
In the night where we belong,
Lost in moments timeless, old,
Night's embrace, both soft and bold.

Silhouette of mountains tall,
Guardians of the night's enthrall,
Bathe in silver, pure and bright,
Glimpses of the mystic night.

As the dawn begins to break,
Dreams and stars at last awake,
Glimpse of night, now fading fast,
Memories of a world so vast.

Twilight's Lullaby

Dusk descends with gentle grace,
Kissing earth in soft embrace,
Colors blend in sky's ballet,
Night prepares for its display.

Birds in chorus, songs they weave,
As the daylight takes its leave,
Twilight sings its lullaby,
Calming hearts as shadows sigh.

Lanterns light the quiet street,
Footsteps soft where lovers meet,
Whispered words and stolen glance,
Nighttime spells a sweet romance.

Moon ascends on silken thread,
Stars emerge from twilight's bed,
Shimmering in cloak of night,
Twilight's lullaby takes flight.

Dreams drift in on whispered lines,
In the dark, a world defined,
Lulled by night's enchanting song,
Twilight's magic lingers long.

Breaking Night

Mountains crowned with twilight hue,
Sky transforming, navy blue,
Stars retreat and fade from sight,
Heralding the breaking night.

Whispers of a breeze unfold,
Stories of the dawn, retold,
Shadows linger, softly part,
Morning's light begins to start.

Owls' calls in echoes cease,
Nighttime's symphony at peace,
First lights cast a golden ray,
Marking the arrival day.

Morning songbirds greet the sun,
Announcing that the night has run,
Petals wake with dewy kiss,
Breaking night, a scene of bliss.

With each breath, a freshened air,
Promise of a day that's fair,
Breaking night, the dawn's delight,
Fading dreams in morning's light.

Evensong Musings

The stars emerge, a silent choir
They twinkle forth, each one inspires
Through velvet skies, a canvas vast
Their luminescence holds us fast

Whispers of wind, a gentle breeze
Rustling leaves in evening's tease
Nature's symphony, at dusk it sings
Of timeless joys and fleeting things

The moon ascends, its silver throne
In solitude, we're not alone
It bathes the night in tender light
Guiding hearts through shadowed flight

Crickets chant their ancient hymns
In twilight's glow, our spirit brims
With gratitude for day's repose
As night bestows its gentle close

Reflection in this quiet hour
Grants our minds a special power
To ponder life, its grand design
In evensong, our souls align

Afterglow Thoughts

The setting sun in crimson hue
Paints the sky in twilight's view
Golden streams on dusky seas
Whisper secrets in the breeze

Memories of the day just passed
In the afterglow, they're cast
Like diamonds scattered in the night
Glimmer soft, but shining bright

Silent fields, the world asleep
In shadows, quiet dreams we keep
We linger in this gentle space
Where time itself slows down its pace

The heart reflects on yesterday
In thoughtful musing, finds its way
To cherish moments that have gone
As night and day together dawn

In the afterglow's embrace
We find a tender, lasting grace
A time to heal, a time to grow
In peace, our deepest thoughts we know

Sundown Reflections

The sun dips low, a fiery fall
Casting shadows long and tall
Mountains blush in evening's gold
A sight to warm both young and old

Silent waters, mirror skies
Reflect the dusk's enchanting guise
Ripples tell a storied past
In currents slow, the moment's vast

Birds take wing to roost on high
Their silhouetted forms goodbye
As daylight fades, night's curtain drawn
We sit and watch till light is gone

Fireflies spark in twilight's gleam
Their dance a flicker, like a dream
Nature's lanterns light the way
Through the velvet touch of day

In sundown's quiet, thoughts arise
To paint reflections in our eyes
A peaceful pause within our stride
Where heart and mind may coincide

Eventide Echoes

Echoes whisper through the pines
In the delicate evening signs
Softly now, the world retires
To the night, with subdued fires

Twilight's sighs, a gentle hymn
Wrap around as light grows dim
Crickets' song, a lullaby
Underneath the moonlit sky

Stars ignite in darkened dome
Guiding sailors, leading home
Their ancient light across the space
Grants the night its sacred grace

Quiet streets and hushed abodes
Eventide's serene crossroads
We breathe in peace, let go of fears
In the echoing of years

Transience in each twilight cast
Reminds us of the days gone past
Yet in its echo, still we find
A lasting echo in the mind

Moonrise Murmurs

In the quiet of the night, the moon ascends
Guiding dreams on silvery bends
Softly murmuring lullabies unheard
Glimmering secrets, no need for words

Beneath her glow, shadows calmly dance
Nighttime whispers, a tranquil romance
Stars align to the moon's gentle tune
Hearts unite under the midnight's boon

The sky, a canvas of celestial art
Carefully painted by a stellar heart
Ethereal beams caressing the earth
Inviting peace, inspiring mirth

Moondust sprinkles in the cool night air
Mystic whispers, a celestial affair
Floating whispers, through dreams they weave
Touching souls, no need to grieve

Tonight's moonrise ends with no sorrow
Promises hopeful dreams of tomorrow
Silent blessings in the lunar light
Guiding us softly through the night

Nightfall Ponderings

As daylight fades, thoughts begin to roam
Seeking shelter in the night's cool dome
Reflections dance on twilight's glass
Moments linger, then slowly pass

Waves of wisdom in the dark sky's fold
Ancient stories, in silence told
Stars above whisper soft advice
Guiding through shadows, calm and precise

Moonlit pathways, thoughts unfurl
Revealing truths in the night's dark swirl
Visions of dreams from nights before
Glimpses of futures, hidden doors

In the quiet, heartbeats slow and still
Mind and soul in the night find their fill
Ephemeral moments, pondering deep
Secrets of the universe, before sleep

Night's embrace with gentle pondering
Silent truths softly wandering
Revelations bloom in the starlit mien
Guiding thoughts in a serene scene

Gloaming Whispers

The world changes as daytime fades
Whispers of dusk serenade glades
Soft hues blend in twilight's slow drift
Bringing peaceful calm as shadows lift

In the gloaming, whispers softly play
As night absorbs the last touch of day
Mysteries unfold in the dim light
Carried on whispers into the night

Nature's secrets surface at twilight's call
Silent voices echo, strange and small
Gloaming whispers wrap the heart in lace
Weaving memories, their soft embrace

As shadows deepen, whispers grow clear
Stories of old, distant yet near
Twilight's curtain slowly comes to close
In whispers' comfort, the night repose

Gloaming's touch with whispered breath
Embraces evening, conquers day's death
Nighttime whispers, dusk's gentle choir
Ignites the heavens with subtle fire

Dusky Epiphanies

At dusk, the world takes on a hue
Shades of twilight born anew
Epiphanies in the softening light
Whispers of day merging with night

Calm unfolds as the sun descends
Bringing thoughts that long transcend
A time of reflection, twilight's grace
Inner truths at dusk, we embrace

The fading sky, a canvas vast
Moments in shadows quietly cast
Epiphanies emerge in evening's sigh
Silent revelations beneath the sky

As the horizon loses its light
Messages unfold in the deepening night
Dusky thoughts with clarity brighten
In the gloaming's glow, spirits lighten

In the dusk, wisdom gently speaks
Mysteries shown in twilight's peaks
Epiphanies in the twilight's seam
Illuminating minds like a gentle dream

Shadowed Ponderings

In twilight's gentle, somber hue,
Unseen thoughts begin to weave,
Fleeting shadows meander through,
Lost in the quiet of the eve.

Murmurs of dusk upon the breeze,
Whispers of secrets now untold,
Under umbra of ageless trees,
An ancient stillness to behold.

Reflections cast in moonlit streams,
Wanderers of forgotten dreams,
A tapestry of silent schemes,
Where every shadow softly gleams.

Glimpses caught in fleeting glance,
A dance of lights and shaded forms,
Within the twilight's tender trance,
A mystery in stillness warms.

Lingering in the veiled night,
Questions in the dark repose,
Gently fades the waning light,
As shadowed pondering grows.

Stars Beyond Horizon

Beyond the reach of setting sun,
A canvas dark, the night begun,
Stars awaken, one by one,
In their eternal, silent run.

Distant fires in cosmic sea,
Jewels scattered carelessly,
Winking in their mystery,
Ancient, vast infinity.

Horizon's edge, a whispered song,
A galaxy's soft siren call,
Where distant wonders all belong,
Tiny beacons mark them all.

A dance of light from far away,
Guiding from astral bays,
Their brilliance in the night shall play,
Ensuring never lost in maze.

To glimpse those lights so far and wide,
Dreamers' hearts are opened wide,
Their hope and longing they'll confide,
In stars beyond the horizon's tide.

Evening Contemplations

At eventide, the world grows still,
Calm descends and hearts refill,
Thoughts begin their inward thrill,
In twilight's gentle, peaceful mill.

The day unwinds its tangled thread,
As dusk enfolds what's left unsaid,
Reflecting on the paths we've tread,
By moonlight softly overhead.

In shadows cast by shading trees,
A hush of night, an endless breeze,
Silent moments, memories seize,
Time itself seems keen to freeze.

Under stars in dark domain,
Thoughts run free, unchained from gain,
Musing with a soft refrain,
Finding solace in the wane.

Thus twilight brings its sweet caress,
A cloak of calm, of thoughtfulness,
Evening's peace, a quiet bless,
Reminding us of gentleness.

Nightfall Serenade

Night whispers with a tender voice,
A serenade to end the day,
Stars in their celestial poise,
Begin their shimmering display.

Winds of evening softly hum,
A lullaby to city scapes,
Nightfall's gentle, soothing drum,
Wraps the world in quiet drapes.

Moonlight spills in silver streams,
Illuminating shadowed dreams,
Weaving through night's gentle themes,
Undisturbed by sunlight's beams.

Crickets' song in symphony,
A harmony of nature's grace,
In night's timeless reverie,
Finds every heart a resting place.

Nightfall serenades the skies,
With melodies both grand and mild,
Underneath its tranquil ties,
The night, a gentle, dreaming child.

Moonlit Fantasies

In fields where shadows gently play,
The moonlight whispers dreams anew,
With silver beams that softly sway,
And paint the night in mystic hue.

Beneath the stars, the night unfolds,
A tapestry of light and grace,
Where every secret gently holds,
A fleeting glimpse of twilight's face.

The winds that breathe a lullaby,
Through trees that sway in tender dance,
Compose a song, a gentle sigh,
That leads the heart to sweet romance.

Dreams woven in the silver glow,
Of moonlit paths and whispered charms,
Guide us where softest rivers flow,
Into the night's embracing arms.

In silent reverie we tread,
On paths where time can lose its stride,
And with the night as our guide,
We wander where the dreams reside.

Velvet Skies

The velvet skies of twilight weave,
A cloak that wraps the day in night,
With stars like pearls, they softly cleave,
The darkness with a gentle light.

Through silent streets, the whispers trail,
Of dreams that drift on silver seas,
And every echo tells the tale,
Of whispered hopes and moonlit pleas.

The world, in softest hues adorned,
Embraces night with shadows deep,
As velvet skies in silence mourned,
The sun's retreat, the moon's slow creep.

In every star, a secret lies,
Of journeys past and dreams reborn,
And as we gaze through velvet skies,
We drift where night's embrace is worn.

With every breath of night's cool air,
We find the peace that day denies,
And in the skies, a world laid bare,
Where endless dreams in silence rise.

Dusky Contemplations

As dusk unfolds its quiet grace,
The world in shadows softly drowns,
With every star that finds its place,
A silent calm the night surrounds.

In twilight's tender, fleeting light,
We ponder on what day's revealed,
The thoughts that come with fall of night,
In dusky hues gently concealed.

The whispers of the evening breeze,
They carry dreams to distant shores,
And with the rustling of the trees,
A song that through the silence soars.

Dusky thoughts, in shadows framed,
They drift like echoes in the dark,
And every fleeting one, unnamed,
Leaves on the night its gentle mark.

Beneath the stars, we find our way,
Through musings deep and silent streams,
In dusky nights, where moments sway,
We weave the fabric of our dreams.

Sunset Echoes

When day descends in hues of fire,
The sunset whispers to the skies,
With every shade a warm desire,
That in the twilight softly lies.

The echoes of a sun's descent,
They linger in the amber light,
And every fleeting moment spent,
Holds whispers of the coming night.

In golden glows, the world is hushed,
As shadows stretch and gently kiss,
The day's farewell in light is brushed,
With tones of evening's tender bliss.

The sky, a canvas painted gold,
Reflects the echoes of the sun,
And as the night begins to fold,
We find that day and night are one.

In sunset's warm and glowing hues,
Memories and dreams align,
And in the twilight's soft refuse,
The echoes of our hearts entwine.

Scarlet Horizon

The sky ablaze, a crimson fire,
Spreading hues as day expires.
Mountains bathed in ruby light,
Nature's stage, a wondrous sight.

Waves reflect a scarlet gleam,
Whispers of a twilight dream.
Birds in chorus sing their song,
As the sun retreats along.

Clouds like lanterns glowing red,
Silent whispers overhead.
Dusk descends with gentle grace,
Scarlet horizon, warm embrace.

Fields of gold beneath the sky,
Evening's kiss, a soft goodbye.
Twilight paints a masterpiece,
Scarlet horizon, heart's release.

Memories in colors bold,
Stories of the day unfold.
Scarlet hues that melt away,
Mark the end of one more day.

Pensive Dusk

Softly falls the evening shade,
Whispered thoughts in twilight's glade.
Silent hours, hearts convene,
In the dusk, a world serene.

Shadows stretch and whispers grow,
Underneath the twilight's glow.
Stars appear, a distant call,
In the night, we find them all.

Silent musings, gentle sway,
Pensive dusk leads thought astray.
Quiet moments gently blend,
In the evening, hearts amend.

Hues of purple grace the sky,
Soft reflections, sight belie.
As the night begins to fall,
In the stillness, we stand tall.

Every thought and every dream,
In this hour, softly gleam.
Pensive dusk, a tranquil veil,
Guides us through the twilight trail.

Nocturnal Echoes

Whispers on the midnight air,
Softly tread without a care.
Moonlight casts a silver glow,
Nocturnal echoes start to grow.

Stars align in velvet dark,
Painting dreams with hopeful spark.
Every shadow hides a song,
In the night where echoes throng.

Crickets hum a gentle tune,
Underneath the watching moon.
Owls call out from distant trees,
Echoes drift upon the breeze.

Night unfolds its secret door,
Whispers lead to something more.
Silent voices, ancient rhyme,
Flow through space and ghostly time.

Hearts attuned to midnight's hush,
In this calm, we never rush.
Nocturnal echoes fill the air,
With their stories pure and rare.

Mystic Evening

Veil of twilight softly falls,
Mystery in every call.
Winds that tell a secret tale,
Mystic evening, whispers pale.

Lanterns float on gentle streams,
Casting lights on wandering dreams.
Fog that curls through ancient trees,
Evening song sung by the breeze.

Every shadow hides its face,
In the twilight's gentle grace.
Eyes that sparkle, hearts that throb,
Evening's magic does its job.

Moonrise paints the heavens high,
Stars like diamonds, sparkling nigh.
Mystic evening's silent show,
Lights a path where few will go.

As the world in slumber lies,
Dreams take wing beneath the skies.
Mystic evening, cloaked in night,
Guides us through with gentle light.

Starlit Meditations

Beneath the vast and silent skies,
The stars begin their lullabies,
In whispers soft, the night replies,
A dream unfolds before our eyes.

Celestial bodies, silent guides,
In constellations, truth resides,
We wander through the cosmic tides,
In starry fields, our thoughts abide.

The moon, a sentinel so bright,
Illuminates the silent night,
In shadows cast, a gentle light,
We find our solace and delight.

Infinite realms of space and time,
Eternal, boundless, so sublime,
In cosmic dance, a sacred rhyme,
We reach beyond the earthly climb.

Thus, in the starlit, cosmic sea,
Our spirits wander, wild and free,
In quiet moments, we decree,
The universe our symphony.

Tales at Sundown

As twilight paints the sky in hues,
The day's last breath in crimson views,
We gather 'round with tales to muse,
In evening's calm, our hearts we choose.

The fire's glow, a gentle gleam,
Reflects upon each wistful dream,
We share our stories, like a stream,
That flows within the twilight's seam.

Ancient myths and legends old,
In whispers soft, their tales unfold,
Of heroes brave and hearts of gold,
In twilight's grasp, the night takes hold.

The stars emerge, a silken veil,
We listen close to every tale,
In evening's lull, our spirits sail,
Where dreams and memories prevail.

Thus, at sundown, we convene,
In shadows cast, our thoughts serene,
With every story, bond unseen,
In evening's grace, our souls are glean.

Evening Solitude

As daylight wanes, the quiet grows,
In evening's hush, a candle glows,
A moment's peace, the heart well knows,
In solitude, the spirit flows.

The world outside fades into grey,
In silent thought, we drift away,
To distant realms where shadows play,
And dreams and whispers softly stay.

A single star, a guiding light,
Emerges in the velvet night,
In solitude, the heart takes flight,
Embracing calm and quiet might.

Within this silent, sacred space,
We find a sense of gentle grace,
A moment's pause, a tender place,
To contemplate the vast embrace.

Evening solitude, profound and deep,
Where whispered secrets softly keep,
In tranquil night's embrace, we steep,
And in our quiet, find our leap.

Gleaming Twilight

In twilight's glow, the world transforms,
A gentle calm, a quiet warms,
The evening breeze, so still, performs,
A dance that quiets life's alarms.

The sky, a canvas painted wide,
With hues that gently coincide,
In twilight's gleam, where dreams reside,
We find our place on eventide.

The sun's last rays, a golden kiss,
Bestow a moment's tender bliss,
In gleaming twilight's soft abyss,
We find a peace we can't dismiss.

Night's curtain drapes the fading day,
In shadows, soft and calm, we lay,
The twilight's whisper softly sway,
In tranquil minds, our fears allay.

And in this gleam, this twilight's light,
We cherish moments pure and bright,
Embraced by evening's gentle might,
We welcome dreams with hearts alight.

Evening Echoes

The sun dips low, a crimson farewell
Whispers of twilight begin to swell
Silhouettes dance in the amber light
Preparing for the embrace of night

Shadows elongate, stretching wide
As stars find their place, side by side
The sky turns to hues of purple and blue
Evening's echoes softly come through

A gentle breeze rustles the leaves
Filling the air with calming reprieves
The world's breath slows, a gentle sigh
As evening echoes bid day goodbye

Moonlight spills like silver streams
Painting the earth with lucid dreams
Crickets sing their sweet refrain
In harmony with the night's domain

With every dusk comes a sacred hush
Colors fade to a tender blush
In the soft embrace of evening's glow
Whispering secrets only night can know

Dusk Resonance

The horizon blushes with a final glow
As the day concludes its radiant show
Colors merge in passionate display
Heralding the end of another day

Trees stand silent, their whispers still
As shadows gather upon the hill
Birds find their rest in twilight's keep
Embraced by the promise of sleep

Night falls softly, a velvet shroud
Wrapping the world in its ebon cloud
The stars begin their ancient dance
Casting spells in a twilight trance

Breezes carry the scent of pine
Through silent valleys and weathered vine
Each sigh of wind, a whispered note
In the symphony dusk has wrote

Amidst the calm, the world serene
Where night and day convene
Lies the resonance of dusk's embrace
A fleeting, yet eternal grace

Silent Nightfall

The silence of night begins to creep
As the world prepares for restful sleep
Shadows whisper secrets of the day
In twilight's tender, muted play

Stars emerge in a sky of midnight hue
Punctuating the silence, crisp and true
Moonlight spills like liquid grace
Touching each corner of this tranquil place

Owl calls echo through the night
A symphony in the absence of light
Crickets join with their gentle song
In nightfall, where we all belong

The breeze holds a breathless calm
Anointing the night with its soothing balm
Every leaf, every blade of grass
Reflects the stillness as moments pass

Within this quiet, the soul finds peace
A serene surrender, sweet release
In silent nightfall, dreams take flight
Etched in the glow of the softest night

Night's Lullaby

Whispered winds through ancient trees
Compose a song with gentle ease
Stars above form a calming roof
Against the sky's dark velvet proof

Moonbeams dance on a silver tide
Guiding the night with arms open wide
Each breath of air sings soft and low
In night's embrace, we gently flow

Crickets chirp their lilting tune
Underneath the watchful moon
Fireflies flicker like fleeting dreams
In harmony with night's soft schemes

Clouds drift slowly, whispering by
Accompanying the night's lullaby
Their shadows move in silent grace
Across the heavens' starlit space

In night's tender, soothing croon
We find calm beneath the moon
Wrapped in the melody of the skies
We rest within night's lullabies

Mysteries at Dusk

The sky an orange hue, the sun dips low,
Whispers in the trees begin to show.
Shadows stretch as daylight starts to fade,
Secrets in the twilight softly laid.

Birds retire, their songs no longer heard,
Leaves rustle faintly, like a whispered word.
Stars peek through the canvas of the night,
Guiding dreams with their celestial light.

Winds carry tales of ancient, distant lands,
Stories written in the shifting sands.
Twilight's magic, a silent, mystic touch,
Unveiling mysteries that tell us much.

Moon rises, casting silver on the ground,
In the stillness, truths and myths abound.
The night descends with promises untold,
Mysteries at dusk, in hues of gold.

Hushed Nightfall

Night descends, a veil of calm and grace,
Stars unveil their beauty in the space.
Moonlight pours upon the sleeping earth,
In hushed nightfall, dreams have their rebirth.

Whispers of the wind through silent trees,
Serenades that waltz upon the breeze.
Oceans mirror the starlit skies above,
Nightfall sings a lullaby of love.

Shadows blend and merge in soft embrace,
Painting pictures in this tranquil place.
In the quiet, stories weave and flow,
Tales of wonders only night can know.

Moments pass in gentle, soothing peace,
All the world seems to find release.
In the hush of nightfall, calm and still,
Time itself obeys the night's sweet will.

Softly fades the echoes of the day,
As darkness guides its gentle, silent way.
In the night, a sacred, quiet call,
Peaceful secrets whispered at nightfall.

Sunset Spirits

Crimson hues ignite the evening sky,
Sunset spirits slowly wave goodbye.
Shadows lengthen, colors start to blend,
Daylight bids farewell, a tender friend.

Golden light that dances on the sea,
Reflects the dreams of what we wish to be.
Mountains bathed in amber's fleeting glow,
As sunset spirits gently come and go.

Twilight's brush paints memories on the air,
Fleeting moments captured everywhere.
Night prepares to weave its darkened cloth,
Sunset spirits blend with evening's froth.

Birds in flight towards the twilight's gate,
Sing their songs, their hearts resonate.
As the sun descends, anew it lifts,
Moments wrapped in sunset's gentle gifts.

Each sunset brings both end and start,
A whispered promise close to every heart.
Spirits rise amidst the fading light,
Guiding us to dreams that take to flight.

Whispers at Dusk

The sky awash with colors, day's last breath,
Whispers at dusk, life beyond death.
Shadows whisper secrets to the night,
In soft whispers, promises take flight.

Leaves murmur softly in the gentle breeze,
Dusk's sweet call, a message in the trees.
Stars begin their soft, unyielding glow,
Whispers at dusk, secrets they bestow.

Crimson fades to purple, night awakes,
In twilight's calm, the heart no longer breaks.
Whispers fly on wings of evening mist,
On the twilight's canvas, gently kissed.

Moments drift in twilight's gentle caress,
Unspoken words that dreams confess.
In the stillness, echoes softly play,
Whispers at dusk lead the way.

Night unfolds its dark embroidered cloak,
In the twilight, dreams and wishes spoke.
Whispers in the dusk both loud and clear,
Guide our hearts as night draws near.

Nighttime Wanderings

Under the star-strewn vault so high,
Where whispers of the night birds fly,
I wander paths where shadows play,
And dreamings of the dusk relay.

Moonlight drapes the sleeping trees,
With tales that drift on midnight breeze,
Softly through the twilight's brush,
Silence holds a gentle hush.

In the quiet, thoughts unfurl,
Dancing in a secret whirl,
Mysteries in the dark abound,
In the night, my heart is found.

Stars above like distant fires,
Kindle ancient, deep desires,
In their light, hope softly glows,
Tracing dreams where no one knows.

Footsteps faint, the owl's decree,
Guides me through eternity,
In the dark, I find my way,
'Neath the stars of night's bouquet.

Ember Glow Reflections

By the hearth, the embers gleam,
Casting shadows like a dream,
Whispers of the flames we know,
In their dance, the stories flow.

Memories in amber light,
Flicker in the cooling night,
Reflections of a day's delight,
Softly held in fire's might.

Glimmers hold a silent tale,
Woven with a midnight veil,
Thoughts arise, in warmth we dwell,
In the glow, all's well to tell.

Voices hushed and eyes aglow,
Share the secrets flames bestow,
In the quiet, hearts confess,
Bound in trust, we acquiesce.

Flames recede, yet linger near,
In their light, we see so clear,
By the hearth, our spirits blend,
In the glow, where worries end.

Night's Stillness

In the stillness of the night,
Stars reflect their ancient light,
Silence wraps the world in peace,
Bidding restless hearts release.

Shadows stride through moonlit beams,
Carrying our quiet dreams,
Each moment, a whispered plea,
Cradled in the dark's decree.

Winds of night, a gentle sigh,
Sweeping 'neath a boundless sky,
Through the hush, a lullaby,
Sings of time that floats on by.

Peaceful night, a sacred dome,
Offering the weary home,
In your calm, we find our rest,
Night's stillness cradles every quest.

Softly falls the velvet night,
Guiding us with tender light,
In the dark, our fears take flight,
Held within the stillness, tight.

Evening Embers

Evening falls with dusky grace,
Tints of dusk on night's embrace,
Fires bloom in fading sun,
As shadows call the day undone.

Embers glow in twilight's grasp,
Holding warmth in gentle clasp,
Their whispers paint the evening air,
With secrets only night would dare.

Crimson hues and darkened gold,
Blend in tales both young and old,
Echoes of the sun's retreat,
Meet the night in silence sweet.

As the stars begin to wake,
Silent vows the night will take,
Ember's glow, a fleeting spark,
Guides us through the coming dark.

Evening embers soft and low,
In their light, all secrets show,
In their warmth, our souls align,
Evening's peace, so pure, divine.

Reflections at Rest

A tranquil mirror, calm and still
Upon the lake, the whispers thrill
Of winds that weave through twilight's veil
In silent dance, the dreams prevail

Moonlight's shimmer on the waves
Glimmer soft, the heart it saves
From daily strife, in peace we dwell
Reflections at rest, a gentle spell

The stars emerge, a cosmic play
Guide us through the night and stay
To whisper secrets, songs of old
In quietude, our thoughts unfold

In nature's silence, find our way
Through night, until the break of day
Embrace the calm, the night so blessed
In reflections, find our spirits dressed

Crepuscular Visions

Twilight paints the skies with hues
Of crimson, orange, violet views
The day dissolves, a softer glow
Crepuscular visions gently flow

The fading light, a whispered sigh
Bids daylight dreams a fond goodbye
The shadows stretch and softly loom
Inviting night, a velvet room

The evening's breath, a gentle breeze
Sways through the leaves, a dance with ease
Soft whispers of the coming night
In twilight's grasp, a brief respite

In the gloaming, hearts find peace
A time to pause, a sweet release
From dawn till dusk, the visions start
To heal the soul and mend the heart

Eve's Quietude

As evening falls and daylight wanes
The sky a canvas, soft refrains
Of dusk's embrace, a tender hold
Eve's quietude, a tale untold

The stars appear, a diamond shroud
Adorning night, their silence loud
A gentle hush across the land
In evening's calm, we understand

The world in slumber, finds its rest
Night's lullaby, a sweet bequest
In shadows deep, our dreams take flight
In Eve's quietude, hearts ignite

The fleeting moments, twilight's kiss
A time of peace, of quiet bliss
In gentle whispers, night ensues
Wrapt in the arms of eve's quietude

Fading Light Reflections

The sun descends, a golden beam
A fleeting dance, a lulling dream
On waves of light, the shadows play
In fading hues, the end of day

The horizon glows, a burning brink
Where sky and sea as one do link
A canvas vast, of fading gold
Reflections deep, the tales unfold

The twilight whispers, soft and low
With every breath, the night does grow
In fading light, our spirits mend
As day's bright fire meets its end

Moon's ascent, the evening's crown
In silent grace, the stars look down
On tranquil seas, a night's embrace
In fading light, find our true place

Milton Keynes UK
Ingram Content Group UK Ltd.
UKHW022139310524
443357UK00004B/91

9 789916 748824